Helping Children See Jesus

ISBN: 978-1-64104-065-5

The New Covenant
New Testament Volume 37: Hebrews, Part Four

Authors: R. Iona Lyster, Doris Stuber Moose, Maureen Pruitt
Illustrator: Frances H. Hertzler
Typesetting and Layout: Patricia Pope

© 2019 Bible Visuals International
PO Box 153, Akron, PA 17501-0153
Phone: (717) 859-1131
www.biblevisuals.org

All rights reserved. No part of this publication may be reproduced, stored in a retrieval system or transmitted in any form by any means, electronic, mechanical, photocopy, recording or otherwise, without the prior permission of the publisher, except as provided by USA copyright law.

RELATED ITEMS

To access related items (such as activities, memory verse posters and translated texts) please visit our webstore at shop.biblevisuals.org and enter 1037 in the search box on the page.

FREE TEXT DOWNLOAD

To access a FREE printable copy of the teaching text (PDF format) in English or other available languages, enter S1037DL in the search box. Add the item to your cart, and use coupon code XTACSV17 at checkout. Once your order is processed you will receive an email with a link to the free download.

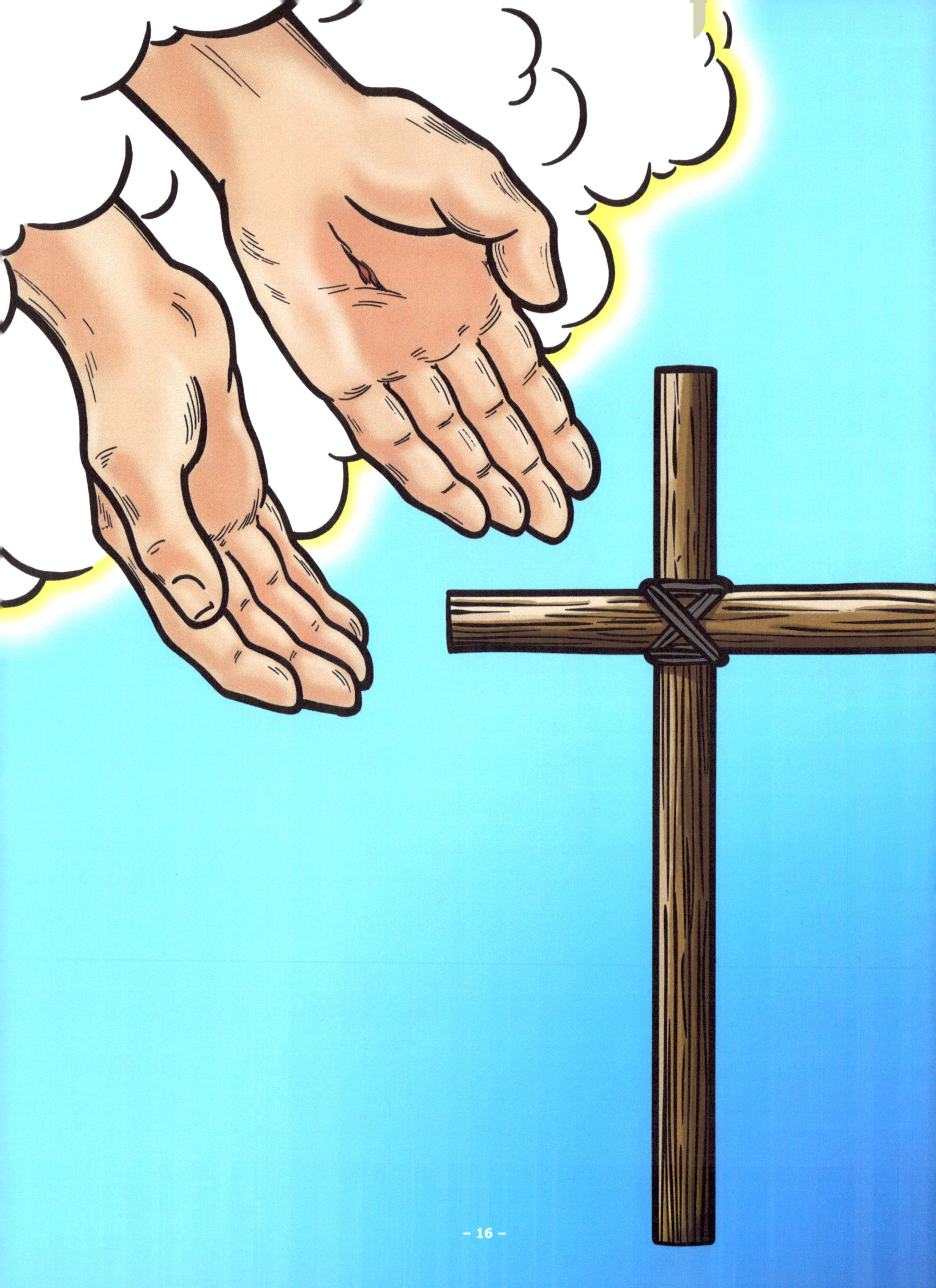

God . . . [Who] brought again from the dead our Lord Jesus . . . through the blood of the everlasting covenant, make you perfect in every good work to do His will.

Hebrews 13:20, 21a

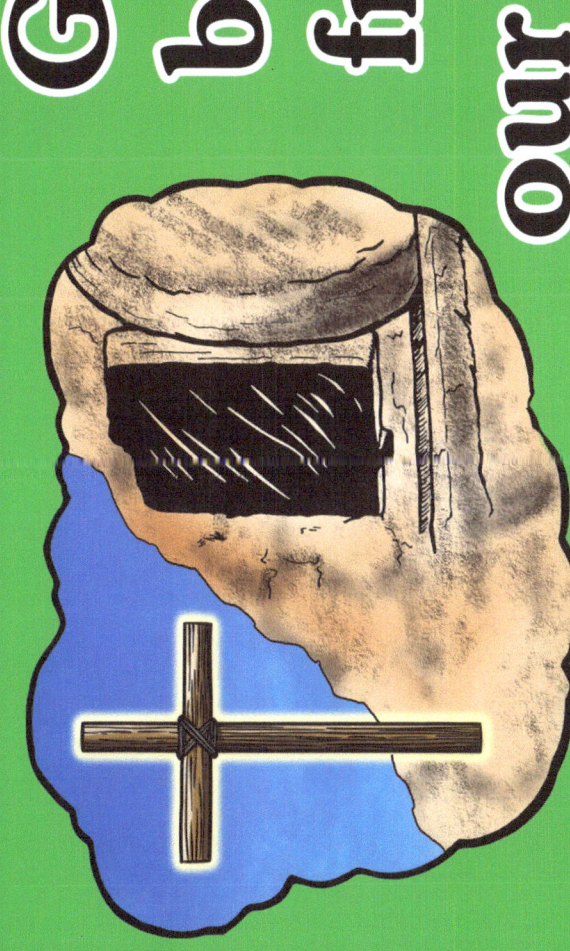

Lesson 1
THE GIVING OF THE OLD COVENANT

NOTE TO THE TEACHER

Early in Bible history, God chose the Jewish nation as a treasure for Himself. For hundreds of years He trained these people through His prophets, angels, priests, Moses, and others. He made a covenant with them. As a result, the Jews [Hebrews] deeply respected all of these–people, angels, the covenant. With the coming of Christ to earth, it was difficult for many Jewish people to understand that the old–though good–had lost its value. Now Jesus alone was to be revered and worshiped. To give instruction in these matters, God addressed to them the book we call *The Epistle to the Hebrews*.

Throughout the letter, the good things of the Jewish faith are contrasted with the better things of Christ. Christ is better than prophets, angels, Moses, Joshua, Aaron. The New Covenant is better than the Old Covenant. (Watch for the word "better.") In this volume we study both the Old and the New Covenants.

The Old Covenant is also referred to as the Mosaic (Moses) Covenant. It is so-called because God spoke the words of the Covenant through His servant Moses, who in turn, gave the Covenant to God's people. God could have spoken directly to His people Himself. Instead, He chose to speak through Moses. For that reason Moses is known as the Mediator of the Old Covenant. He is the one who goes between God and man. ("Mediator" means go-between.)

A covenant is an agreement between two or more parties. The Old Covenant was between God and the Jewish people. It was conditional. That is to say, IF the Israelites (another name for Jews or Hebrews) would keep the Law which God gave them, GOD would keep His promises of blessing to them. (See Exodus 19:5-6.) The Israelites agreed to obey God's commands, saying, "All that the Lord has spoken, we will do." (See Exodus 19:8; 24:3, 7; Deuteronomy 5:27.) Alas, they failed! (See Deuteronomy 5:29.) This, of course, was no surprise to God. He knew they would fail. Years later, therefore, He promised to make a New Covenant with them. (See Jeremiah 31:31-34.) That New Covenant (referred to in Hebrews 8:10-12) is unconditional. God tells what He by Himself will do. And that is that! We begin this volume with a study of the Old Covenant.

In the opening illustration of this lesson, use names and sports (or games) that are familiar to your people. If they are acquainted with the Olympics, use that as the example.

Scripture to be studied: Exodus 19:1-20:26; 24:1-8; 34:29-32; Hebrews 8:6-13; 9:1-15, 18-22

The *aim* of the lesson: To show that although the people in Moses' day continually failed God, Christian believers now have power to obey Him.

What your students should *know*: That believers have the Holy Spirit to enable them to obey God.

What your students should *feel*: A keen desire to please God.

What your students should *do*: Trust the Holy Spirit to give them the power to do what God wants them to do.

Lesson outline (for the teacher's and students' notebooks):

1. The old covenant given by God (Exodus 19:3-6; 20:1-7).
2. The old covenant–given through a mediator (Exodus 19:17; 20:19; 24:2-4; 34:29-32).
3. The old covenant–sealed with blood. (Exodus 24:6-8; Hebrews 9:18-22).
4. The old covenant was temporary (Hebrews 8:6-13).

The verses to be memorized:

God . . . [Who] brought again from the dead our Lord Jesus . . . through the blood of the everlasting covenant, make you perfect in every good work to do His will.

(Hebrews 13:20, 21a)

THE LESSON

Let us suppose that the men of our village are invited to have a contest with men from nearby villages. We are to choose two good swimmers, two runners, two who can jump high, and two who can throw a javelin (or a spear or boomerang). After days of discussion, the decision is made. It looks like this:

Best swimmer: JOSE	*Best runner:* JOSE
Second best: CARLOS	*Second best:* PIETRO
Best jumper: JOSE	*Best thrower:* JOSE
Second best: TOMAS	*Second best:* SILAS

Carlos, Pietro, Tomas, Silas are good. But Jose is better. And he is better in everything.

Just so, the book of Hebrews teaches that the Jewish prophets, angels, priests, and Moses were good. God used them for particular purposes–but only until the Lord Jesus Christ came to earth. Now He, God the Son, is better than prophets. He is better than angels. He is better than priests. He is better than Moses. Indeed, He is best of all. These truths have been made clear in our study of Hebrews. Today we shall learn that He is also a better Mediator of a better Covenant. Do the words Mediator and Covenant sound like a foreign language to you? Listen carefully!

A "covenant" is an agreement. It may be a conditional agreement. For example, a father may say, "I will take you for a boat ride on Saturday if you empty the trash every day this week." (***Teacher:*** Mention a treat and chores that apply to your group.) If the boy declares, "I'll do it," they have made a conditional covenant. IF the boy does what his father commands, he gets the boat ride. That is the condition of the agreement. On Monday, Tuesday, Wednesday, and Thursday he takes out the trash. Friday he does not.

Early Saturday morning, he hops out of bed and rushes to his father. "Get up, Dad!" he says. "Today we go on the boat ride."

"Sorry, son," his father answers. "No boat ride today. You broke the covenant." Because the boy failed to keep his part of the agreement, the conditional covenant is broken.

The father could have promised at the beginning of the week, "Son, on Saturday I'll take you for a boat ride." The boy is not required to do anything. This would have been an UNconditional covenant or agreement.

Two of the most important covenants ever made were between God and His treasured people, the Israelites. One was called "the Old Covenant;" the other, "the New Covenant." We shall learn about the new one later. First, we must completely understand the Old Covenant.

In the Old Covenant, God agreed to do certain special things for the Israelites IF they agreed to obey Him. This was a conditional covenant. The people were free to say, "No," or to say, "Yes, we agree to the plan. We promise to obey all Your rules." This latter is exactly what they said. (See Exodus 19:5-8.)

At the time of this agreement, God's people were traveling in the wilderness from Egypt to their homeland, Canaan. Try to think what might have happened in their camp that day. Could it have been like this?

1. THE OLD COVENANT –GIVEN BY GOD
Exodus 19:3-6; 20:1-7

Show Illustration #1

"Iddo, come!" his father commanded. "You must help clean the camp."

"Yes, Father," Iddo replied. "But why is everyone rushing?"

"Three days from now, God Himself is going to come down to speak to us. He told Moses, our leader, that we must wash our clothes. (See Exodus 19:10, 14.) Everything must be clean for Him, for He is holy."

Iddo was puzzled. "You have said that God is Spirit, Father. How shall we know He is here?"

"When we hear a trumpet, we are to gather near Mount Sinai. But we dare not go up the mountain or even touch the edge of it. He will be there, even though we cannot see Him."

Iddo was full of questions. "Did Moses say why God wants to talk to us?"

"Yes, Iddo. He said God has chosen us as His special nation. We are to be holy people set apart for Him. He wants to make a covenant–an agreement–with us. We have already told Moses that we agree to do all God says. Now God is ready to give us His laws." (See Exodus 19:5-8.)

On the morning of the third day, a thick cloud covered the mountain. Thunder rolled! Lightning flashed! The trumpet sounded! Moses brought the trembling people out of camp to meet with God. Smoke rose from the mountain! Fire blazed! The whole mountain shook! The trumpet sounded louder and louder! And God called Moses to the top of the mountain.

Moses returned shortly with a strict warning: "Don't break through the boundaries trying to see God. If you do, you will die!"

The Israelites, shivering with fear, moved farther from the mountain.

2. THE OLD COVENANT GIVEN THROUGH A MEDIATOR
Exodus 19:17; 20:19; 24:2-4; 34:29-32

Moses continued, "God is waiting for me at the mountain top. I must return now. Stay away from the mountain!"

"Yes, yes!" the people chorused. "God has shown us His glory and His greatness. We have heard His voice out of the fire. We have seen that God talks with man . . . If we hear the voice of the LORD our God any more, we shall die . . . You go, Moses, and hear everything the LORD our God says. Then you can tell us and we shall hear and do it." (See Deuteronomy 5:24-27.)

"Iddo," his father whispered, "Moses is our mediator–our go-between. God is perfect and pure and holy. We have washed our clothes and cleaned our camp. But our lives are not clean and pure and holy. We are too sinful to talk with God or have Him talk directly to us. Moses is talking to God for us, telling Him we have agreed to obey His covenant. Now God will tell him what we must do. Moses, in turn, will tell us. We could not know the commands of God without a mediator."

God gave Moses many commands and rules on the mountain top. The rules told the people how to worship God and how to act toward other people. There were ten commandments, beginning with, "You must not worship any other god but Me . . . You must not make or worship any idol." . . . One said, "You must not murder." Another, "You must not steal." Then, "You must not lie."

Finally, "You must not want what belongs to someone else."

Show Illustration #2

There was much, much more. Finally Moses, the mediator, came down from the mountain. He told the people what God had commanded. When they heard the laws and rules, the Israelites again promised, "All the words which the LORD has said, we shall do" (Exodus 24:3). God and Israel were in agreement. The covenant was made.

3. THE OLD COVENANT–SEALED WITH BLOOD
Exodus 24:6-8; Hebrews 9:18-22

There was so much to be remembered that Moses wrote it all in a book–the Book of the Covenant. (See Exodus 24:7; compare 2 Kings 23:2. (*Teacher:* In the earlier days of Israel's history, stone was often used for books. In illustration #2 we have used large stones, though the Book of the Covenant may have been written on a scroll. Remember: the Book of the Covenant contained all of Exodus 20, 21, 22, and 23.)

Show Illustration #3

The next morning Moses arose early and built an altar. He sent some of the young men to kill animals for sacrifices to the Lord. Then Moses sprinkled half of the sacrificial blood on the altar. Taking the Book of the Covenant, he again read God's commands and rules to the people. Again the Israelites agreed, "All that the LORD has said we shall do, and be obedient" (Exodus 24:7).

Immediately Moses sprinkled the Book of the Covenant and all the people, saying, "See the blood of the covenant, which the Lord has made with you." (See Exodus 24:8; Hebrews 9:19-20.) The blood sealed the covenant, making it secure.

The people of God understood that they would have His blessing IF they obeyed His laws. Three times they insisted they would do this.

4. THE OLD COVENANT WAS TEMPORARY
Hebrews 8:6-13

God again called, "Moses, come up to Me on the mountaintop. I have written My commands on tablets of stone. You can teach them to My people." Moses went up into God's glory cloud at the top of Mount Sinai. There he received two stone tablets. On them God had written His commandments. (See Exodus 31:18.)

Because Moses was gone many days, God's people became restless. To Aaron (Moses' brother) they said, "Moses, our leader, has disappeared. Something must have happened to him. Make us a god to lead us."

Imagine that! The first two commands in the Covenant were, "You must not worship any other god but Me." And, "You must not make or worship any idol." Three times the Israelites had agreed to obey all the laws and commands. Now, with their own lips, they asked for another god–an idol.

"Give me your golden earrings," Aaron ordered. From them he made a golden calf. And the people whom God had chosen for His special treasure, turned from Him to the calf god. They had failed to keep their part of the covenant.

Show Illustration #4

Moses rushed down the mountain, carrying the commandments which God Himself had written on stone. Seeing the people dancing before the calf, Moses angrily smashed the tablets to the ground. (*Teacher:* Observe, please, that the tablets in the illustration are large. Later, when Moses made duplicate tablets of stone, he took them "in his hand"–not "hands." See Exodus 34:1-4. Those in the illustration are purposely larger so your students may see them easily.)

This was only the beginning. In the years that followed the people broke God's laws many, many times. God often became angry with them and might have destroyed them. But Moses, the mediator, would go between the people and God asking His forgiveness. So it was for years and years. God always kept His part of the Covenant. His people continued to fail. They needed–and will receive some day–a New Covenant. We shall learn about this in future lessons.

Today, Christian believers can obey God. For God gives his own a wonderful helper, the Holy Spirit. He lives within them teaching the right way to live. He makes them feel bad when they do wrong. He gives them power to do right. If you have placed your trust in the Lord Jesus but are not obeying God, you are sinning. Will you confess that sin to God right now? "He that covereth his sins shall not prosper: but whoso confesseth and forsaketh them shall have mercy" (Proverbs 28:13). Will you promise God that you will do what He wants you to do? Will you write that promise in your notebook?

Lesson 2
CHRIST AND THE OLD COVENANT

NOTE TO THE TEACHER

The Jewish Christians who received *The Epistle to the Hebrews* had problems. For 1500 years their fathers and their fathers' fathers had studied God's Law. From the Law they had learned the right way to live. Because God had promised to bless them IF they obeyed Him, they had covenanted (agreed) to do what He commanded. Quickly, however, they failed–and kept on failing. They offered countless sacrifices for their sins. Continually they needed someone to be their mediator–to go between them and God.

Then the Lord Jesus came to earth, died, rose again, and ascended to heaven. Now everything was different. God instructed the Hebrew Christians (in their letter) that Christ, His Son, is better than all the angels, people, and things that the Jewish people had loved and respected. This was hard for them to understand. They had enjoyed their position as God's special people. They loved to talk of their famous ancestors: Abraham, Isaac, Jacob. They were proud of their beautiful temple worship, so different from the worship of other nations. Having become Christians, they had lost their extra-ordinary identity. This was a problem to them.

However, in this same letter, God assured His people that at some future day they will receive a New Covenant. According to the terms of that agreement, all Jews (who trust in His Son) will again be His special people. (See Hebrews 8:10-12.)

The parable of our Lord (used in this lesson) was familiar to the Jewish people. The Prophet Isaiah had spoken of Israel as a vineyard more than 700 years earlier. (See Isaiah 5:1-7.) Because they understood what Christ meant, the Jewish leaders determined to kill Him. (See, for example, Luke 20:19.) The sinless, obedient Son of God would be slain by sinful men who could not–would not–obey God. Think of that!

Scripture to be studied: Mark 12:1-13; Hebrews 10:1-22

The *aim* of the lesson: To show that Christ perfectly obeyed God always.

What your students should *know*: That the Lord Jesus Christ gives His own the power to obey God.

What your students should *feel*: Such love for God that they will want to obey Him always.

What your students should *do*: Because of their love for God (not fear of Him), determine what they can do today (and this week) in obedience to Him.

Lesson outline (for the teacher's and students' notebooks):
1. The Israelites (God's chosen people) disobeyed God and hated His Son (Mark 12:1-13; compare Matthew 21:33-46; Luke 20:9-19; Isaiah 5:1-7).
2. The sadness of Christ because of the broken covenant (Matthew 23:37-39; Luke 13:34-35; Luke 19:41-44).
3. Christ always obeyed God perfectly (Luke 2:52; Matthew 4:1-11; John 8:29; Hebrews 5:7-9).
4. As Christ proved His love for God by obeying Him, so must we (Matthew 26:39; John 14:15, 21-23; 15:10; 1 John 5:3).

The verses to be memorized:

God . . . [Who] brought again from the dead our Lord Jesus . . . through the blood of the everlasting covenant, make you perfect in every good work to do His will.

(Hebrews 13:20, 21a)

THE LESSON

Suppose you knew that someone hated you so much he wanted to kill you. If he had no reason for hating you, how would you feel towards him? (*Teacher:* Encourage class discussion.)

This was exactly the experience of the Lord Jesus. He did good things for many people. He lived a pure, perfect life. He always obeyed God in everything. Although He was a Jew, He was fiercely hated by the Jews–the nation God had chosen as His special treasure.

When the Lord Christ was on earth, He could have asked God to punish the Jews for their hatred. He could have spoken angrily to them. Instead, He simply told them a parable. A parable is a story of everyday life which teaches another truth. The other meaning of the story was perfectly clear to the Jewish leaders. Because He told the story of a vineyard and because God had spoken of Israel (the Jews) as a vineyard (See Isaiah 5:1-7), they understood He was speaking of them.

1. THE ISRAELITES (GOD'S CHOSEN PEOPLE) DISOBEYED GOD AND HATED HIS SON
Mark 12:1-13; compare Matthew 21:33-46; Luke 20:9-19; Isaiah 5:1-7

This was the parable Jesus told: A man planted grape vines (a vineyard). To protect the young vines, he planted a row of bushes around the vineyard. He rented the land to some farmers and went away. The Bible does not give the full details, but apparently the man made this covenant (agreement) with the farmers: "You may use the vineyard and keep most of the grapes, IF you let me have some of them." What kind of covenant was this? *(A conditional covenant)* Immediately, the farmers agreed. They tended the grapes carefully. At harvest time, there was a large crop of good grapes.

Show Illustration #5

One day, according to the covenant, the owner sent a servant to the farmers. "I have come for my master's grapes," the servant said. The farmers grabbed him, beat him severely, and sent him off without any grapes.

So the owner sent another servant to collect what really belonged to him. The farmers beat that servant about the head, and sent him back emptyhanded. Others, too, were beaten. Still others were killed!

Having sent all his servants, the owner decided to send his beloved son. They will respect and honor my son, he thought.

When the farmers saw him coming, they exclaimed, "Look! It is the son of the owner. Some day this vineyard will belong to him. Let us kill him so he cannot receive it. Then it will be ours." So they threw the son out of the vineyard and killed him. (See Matthew 21:39.)

How do you suppose the owner of the vineyard felt when he learned what they had done to his son? What do you think he did? (Encourage class discussion.)

The Lord Jesus said the owner completely destroyed those wicked farmers. Then he made a new covenant with others who could be trusted to give him his fruit.

When the leaders of the nation of Israel heard this parable, they became angry. What the Lord Jesus meant was perfectly clear to them. They, the Jews, were the vineyard. They belonged to their Owner, God, who had chosen them and set them apart for a special purpose. As the vineyard was protected by the bushes around it, so His people were protected by God's laws and commands. Alas, the people who had gladly agreed to obey God, disobeyed Him. So God sent prophets (His servants) to ask for fruit (their obedience). But the Israelite leaders (like the wicked farmers) hated the prophets. They mistreated some and killed others. (*Teacher:* Elijah, for example, had to run for his life, 1 Kings 19:1-3. Jeremiah was cast into prison, Jeremiah 37:15-16. Zechariah was stoned, 2 Chronicles 24:20-21. John the Baptist was beheaded, Mark 6:27.)

The Lord Jesus also told the Jewish people (in the parable) something that would happen in the future. The Owner (God), He said, has sent the Son of His love (Jesus Christ) to His people (Israel). They will kill Him (as the farmers killed the owner's son). For this reason, God will turn from His treasured people for a while. (See Romans 11:1-25.) Because Jesus spoke the truth, the Jews hated Him. (See Luke 20:19-20.)

2. THE SADNESS OF CHRIST BECAUSE OF THE BROKEN COVENANT
Matthew 23:37-39; Luke 13:34-35; Luke 19:41-44

The Lord Jesus knew of their hatred, of course. Still He loved them. Shortly after telling the parable, He stood on a high place looking over their capital city, Jerusalem. He saw their magnificent temple of worship. He thought of God's people, the Jews, who were continually disobeying God.

Show Illustration #6

"O Jerusalem! O God's people!" He cried. "You stone and kill God's servants who are sent to tell you the right way. How often I have wanted to teach you, comfort you, protect you as a hen does when she gathers her chicks under her wings! But you would not let Me." (See Luke 13:34-35.)

Thinking about the way the Jewish people would continue to turn away from Him, Jesus had to tell them some bad news. "Your wonderful city will be left in ruins. (See Matthew 23:38; 24:1-2.) You'll have to be destroyed as the wicked farmers were who murdered the servants and the son."

And this is exactly what happened. Less than 40 years later, God allowed their enemies, the Romans, to march into their city. Great stone buildings and their beautiful temple were smashed and left in heaps, and many Jews were killed. God allowed them to be punished. Why? Because they had broken their part of the covenant. Originally, they had agreed to worship God alone. They had agreed to obey Him always. But they failed and kept on failing. They had turned from the One who wanted to be a kind, loving Father to them.

3. CHRIST ALWAYS OBEYED GOD PERFECTLY
Luke 2:52; Matthew 4:1-11; John 8:29; Hebrews 5:7-9

One alone obeyed God's commands perfectly. Jesus, God's own beloved Son, came to earth to do His Father's will, the Letter to the Hebrews says. (See Hebrews 10:7, 9.)

Show Illustration #7

Satan, the great tempter himself, wanted Jesus to turn from God. He offered to give Jesus the kingdoms of the world if He (Christ) would worship him (Satan). Jesus answered with the words of God: "You shall worship the Lord your God, and Him only you shall worship" (Matthew 4:9-10). He would not disobey God.

When Satan told Jesus to make some bread out of stones, Jesus said, "No!" He had no food and was very hungry. But it was not God's will for Him to make bread out of stones. So He would not do it. Because He is One with God, Jesus did not–could not–sin. During His 33 years on earth, He always did right and obeyed God perfectly. (See Luke 2:52; John 15:10b.)

It helps to know that Jesus understands perfectly what it is like to be sad, hungry, thirsty, tempted. Though He is in heaven today, He knows exactly how we feel. (See Hebrews 2:18; 4:15.)

4. AS CHRIST PROVED HIS LOVE FOR GOD BY OBEYING HIM, SO MUST WE
Matthew 26:39; John 14:15, 21-23; 15:10; 1 John 5:3

In His human body, Jesus dreaded the lashings, pain and His death of the cross. But there was no other way to save the world.

Show Illustration #8

So in Gethsemane Garden, Jesus prayed to His Father, "Not My will, but Yours be done." He was willing to obey because of love, love for God and love for us. By dying on the cross, He would provide eternal salvation for all the world. For this reason He accepted His torturous death with joy. (See Hebrews 12:2.) Think of that!

The Bible says that we, like the Jews of old, are disobedient. We are all sinners, because of the disobedience of Adam. Each of us is born with a sinful nature and we choose to sin. By ourselves, we have no power to obey God. But the moment we place our trust in the Lord Jesus Christ, we have His eternal life in us. (See Hebrews 5:9.) It is His life that makes us want to obey God, as He did. (See Matthew 26:39; Philippians 2:8; Hebrews 5:8.)

We obey God by obeying our leaders and doing what they say. God tells us to do this. (See Hebrews 13:17.) Children obey God when they obey and honor their parents. (See Ephesians 6:1; Colossians 3:20.) Servants obey God by obeying those for whom they work. (See Ephesians 6:5-8; Colossians 3:22-24; Titus 2:9.) A wife disobeys God if she refuses to obey her husband. She causes people to speak against the Word of God. (See Titus 2:5.) We obey God when we take hold of our thoughts and make them obey Christ. (See 2 Corinthians 10:5.) Are you an obedient Christian? Do you obey the commands of God because you love Him?

How does God want you to obey Him today? this week? Write in your notebook what you purpose to do. Then we shall pray together, asking God to help you to obey Him lovingly.

Lesson 3
GOD PROMISES A NEW COVENANT

NOTE TO THE TEACHER

About 1,400 years before the coming of Christ to earth, God made a temporary, conditional covenant with the nation of Israel. God promised to bless the people He had chosen as His treasure IF they would obey Him and worship Him alone. Alas, the Hebrews failed and kept on failing. About 700 years later, God promised through the Prophet Isaiah that He would make a New Covenant with His people. This would be an everlasting covenant, God said. (See Isaiah 61:8b.) A hundred years later (about 600 BC), God repeated His promise. This New Covenant, He said, would be an unconditional covenant.

Instead of writing His laws on stone (as in the Old Mosaic Covenant), He would write them on the hearts of His people. (See Jeremiah 31:31-34; compare Hebrews 8:10.)

The New Covenant is more effective than the Old. The laws in the Old Covenant showed what sin was, but did not take it away. (See Romans 8:3-4; Hebrews 7:19.) The New Covenant is sealed by the blood of the Lord Jesus Christ. (See Matthew 26:27-28; 1 Corinthians 11:25; Hebrews 9:11-12, 18-23.) Under the New Covenant, a repentant Israel will be established forever. God promises that a day will come (a day which is yet in the future) when many Israelites will receive the Lord Jesus as Saviour. Then they will have God's special blessing. (See Jeremiah 31:31-40; 2 Samuel 7:10-16.) What a wonderful day that will be!

Scripture to be studied: Isaiah 61:8b; Jeremiah 31:31-34; Philemon 1-25; Hebrews 9:11-22; Luke 22:14-20

The *aim* of the lesson: To show that the New Covenant and forgiveness of sins are guaranteed by the blood of Christ.

What your students should *know*: That there are blessings right now for all who trust in Christ.

What your students should *feel*: Thanksgiving for the blessings they have received through the blood of Christ.

What your students should *do*: Search the Scriptures daily to find the blessings that are theirs.

Lesson outline (for the teacher's and students' notebooks):
1. An unconditional covenant is needed (Hebrews 10:4, 11).
2. An eternal Mediator is needed (Philemon 10-18; Hebrews 7:25)
3. The New Covenant is sealed and thus guaranteed by the blood of Christ (Matthew 26:28; Hebrews 9:15).
4. Blessings because of the New Covenant (Hebrews 7:25; 9:12; 12:5-10; 13:5-6, 20-21).

The verses to be memorized:

God . . . [Who] brought again from the dead our Lord Jesus . . . through the blood of the everlasting covenant, make you perfect in every good work to do His will.

(Hebrews 13:20, 21a)

THE LESSON

Have you ever gone on a treasure hunt? Was hunting easy or hard? What were you looking for? Tigers? Oil? Elephants? Gold? Diamonds? Bears? Food? After finding your treasure, what did you do with it? (*Teacher:* Encourage discussion.)

In the Word of God are all kinds of treasures. Some we can find quite easily. Others are found only by searching. And searching, like hunting, is not easy. Hebrews, the book which we have been studying, is rich with treasures. If you are not

Jewish, you may have to work hard to understand some of its wonderful truths. But when you find them, you will want to list them in your notebook. Best of all, God's treasures can affect your life. Listen carefully!

1. AN UNCONDITIONAL COVENANT IS NEEDED
Hebrews 10:4, 11

God and the Israelites made a covenant. The people of Israel wanted God to keep His part of the covenant. They wanted Him to bless them with all kinds of good things. They wanted His help and protection. But they did not keep their part of the agreement. They refused to obey Him completely and worship Him alone.

Show Illustration #9

God sent personal reminders to them. He chose special messengers (called prophets) to give His message to the people. The prophets reminded the Jewish people to obey God. They warned them that they would be punished for their disobedience.

For hundreds of years the people of God did the same things over and over again: (1) They refused to obey God and, instead, worshiped false, make-believe gods. (2) They were punished by God. (3) They told God they were sorry and turned back to the right way, worshiping Him only. (4) They were forgiven by God and He blessed them with good things. Then back to (1) disobedience, (2) punishment, (3) repentance, and (4) forgiveness, time after time. (See Hebrews 10:4, 11.) They simply did not–could not–keep their part of the Old Covenant.

Because of God's great love, He promised to give the Jews a New Covenant. The Prophet Jeremiah told them it would be a different kind of covenant. It would not depend upon their obedience. Instead, the New Covenant would all depend upon God Himself. God even let His people know–hundreds of years beforehand–that His Son would come to earth. He would be the One who would make the New Covenant possible.

All of Israel should have jumped for joy! They should have watched eagerly for the coming of the Son of God. Instead, when He came (hundreds of years later), they did not welcome him.

Show Illustration #5

Just as the farmers killed the son of the vineyard owner, so the Jews hated God's Son and put Him to death. No wonder God had to punish the nation. He allowed an enemy army (the Romans) to march in and destroy Jerusalem, tearing down their magnificent temple of worship. And, exactly as the Lord Jesus had foretold, many Jewish people were killed and the rest had to escape from their homeland. Today, almost 2,000 years later, they are still scattered throughout the world.

2. AN ETERNAL MEDIATOR IS NEEDED
Philemon 10-18; Hebrews 7:25

The first time God made a covenant with His special people, Moses was the mediator. He was the man in the middle. He was chosen to go between God and man. He would listen to God's words, then give them to the people. He would also hear the words of the people and take them to God. After Moses, there were many more mediators. (For example, the priests were mediators.) All went between God in heaven and people on earth.

But the great preacher and missionary, Paul, who wrote much of our New Testament, once did the work of another kind of mediator. He went between two men here on earth.

At the time, Paul was in prison for preaching about Jesus. There he met a man named Onesimus. Onesimus was a sinner–and he knew it. He was a slave who had run away from his master. In those days, this was a crime for which he would have been put to death. When Paul explained to Onesimus that he should place his trust in Christ as his Saviour, Onesimus did so. He turned about completely. Now that Onesimus was a Christian, what should he do? Return to his master? Even if it meant being killed? (*Teacher:* Have class discussion.) Onesimus needed a mediator. He needed someone to go between him and his master.

Show Illustration #10

Paul said, "Onesimus, I cannot leave this prison and go to Philemon, your master. But I shall write a letter to him." Which is exactly what Paul did. In the letter he explained that Onesimus had become a Christian and was like a son to him (Paul). Paul wrote, "Receive him as a Christian brother. Forgive him for the wrong he has done." Paul was doing the work of a mediator–going between the sinner and the one he had sinned against.

Paul added, "If Onesimus owes you anything, send the bill to me. I will repay you." He became responsible for Onesimus debts, promising to pay for them. What a good go-between he was!

Have you ever been a mediator? If so, what did you learn from the experience? (*Teacher:* If the discussion of your students reveals that they do not clearly understand the meaning of "mediator," please give additional help.)

Hundreds of mediators went between God and people during the time of the Old Covenant. Although many of them were good men, all had sinful natures. Each needed to offer sacrifices for his own sins before sacrificing for the sins of others. (See Hebrews 7:27.) Each mediator served a while–then died.

So God provided a better Mediator–the perfect One. This Mediator lives forever and ever. He understands people. He is like God. Indeed, He is God the Son. He is now the one and only Mediator between God and people. (See John 14:6; 1 Timothy 2:5; Hebrews 7:23-28.) Because the Lord Jesus Christ is sitting next to God in heaven, He can talk to God for us all the time. (See Hebrews 7:25; 10:12.)

3. THE NEW COVENANT IS SEALED AND GUARANTEED BY THE BLOOD OF CHRIST
Matthew 26:28; Hebrews 9:15

According to the laws of the Old Covenant, each person had to give an animal (or bird) sacrifice before he worshiped God. The sacrifice died for the sins of the worshiper. The blood of the sacrifice covered the sins of the person who gave it. Soon, however, that person sinned again. Then another sacrifice had to be made. Hundreds–even thousands–of animals died, according to the rules of the Old Covenant.

But the blood of animals was not good enough for the New Covenant. There had to be one perfect sacrifice. It would have to last forever.

Show Illustration #11

This is what the Lord Jesus taught His disciples the night before He died. They were seated about a table. Breaking some bread into pieces, Jesus said, "This is My body, given for you." He meant that His body would be torn. He Himself would die for them. Then He raised a cup, saying, "This is My blood of the New Covenant. It is given for the forgiveness of sins." (See Matthew 26:28; Mark 14:24; Luke 22:20. In these verses, as in Hebrews 9:15, the word "testament" should be translated "covenant" instead.) He wanted them to know beforehand that He, God the Son, would give His life-blood for the sins of the world. His blood, instead of simply covering sin, would rescue them from its penalty forever. (See Hebrews 9:15.)

The next day, instead of offering the blood of an animal sacrifice, the Lord Jesus gave His own blood. When He died on the cross, the Old Covenant was over. In its place was the New Covenant, sealed with the blood of the Mediator Himself.

4. BLESSINGS BECAUSE OF THE NEW COVENANT
Hebrews 7:25; 9:12; 12:5-10; 13:5-6, 20-21

Now the way to God was wide open for the whole world. Jesus died once and He died for all. Today, anyone–Jew or non-Jew–who believes that Christ Jesus is God the Son, places his trust in Christ, and turns from his sins, becomes a member of the family of God. And those in God's family are His special treasured people. (See Titus 2:14; 1 Peter 2:9.)

Show Illustration #12

According to God's New Covenant, there is a wonderful future ahead. (We shall study about that in our next lesson.) But right now there are marvelous blessings for all who have trusted in Christ. These treasures will be found by those who study the Bible. And the truths they find will affect their lives. For example, in the book of Hebrews, we learn that:

1. Because the Lord Jesus Christ lives forever, He is praying for His own right now. (See Hebrews 7:25; 9:24; 10:12; 12:2.) He is our Mediator. (Because He prays, we too should pray.)
2. With His own blood, Christ paid for our sins and made our eternal salvation sure. (See Hebrews 9:12.) He is our Saviour, our Redeemer. (Have you given yourself for Christ who gave Himself for you?)
3. God trains and punishes His own as a father trains and punishes his child. By accepting His training, we share His holiness. (See Hebrews 12:5-10.) He is our heavenly Father. (Is your life improving because of God's discipline?)
4. Children of God have nothing to fear, for the Lord never leaves His own. (See Hebrews 13:5-6.) He is our Companion and Helper. (Are you a courageous child of God?)
5. As a shepherd provides for his sheep, so the Lord Jesus (by the blood of the everlasting New Covenant) gives His children all they need for doing what He wants. (See Hebrews 13:20-21.) He is our Great Shepherd. (Are you doing what the Shepherd wants you to do?)

Are you studying God's Word each day? When you find some wonderful truth, do you mark it in your Bible or write it in your notebook? Remember this: no matter how many marvelous things you find, there are still many, many more. And all will help your Christian growth. You can be a full-grown Christian only by studying the Word of God. Are you willing to do this?

Lesson 4
THE NEW COVENANT FULFILLED

NOTE TO THE TEACHER

As we study these lessons on the New Covenant, we learn how much we owe our Lord Jesus Christ. He is the one and only Mediator who brings man to God. He is the Redeemer who paid our debt of sin. He, the perfect sacrifice, gave His own blood to cleanse our sins.

In the previous volume on Hebrews, we studied about Christ's being our Great High Priest. He is alive forever, and is now at the right hand of God to pray for us. When we sin, He is there to restore our fellowship with God. When we call for help, He gives us power to overcome temptation. Because He is a man, He fully understands all our needs, our temptations, our problems. He is able to sympathize with our weaknesses because of the trials He had on earth.

The Hebrew Christians to whom this letter was written, knew of the priesthood of Aaron. They were familiar with the sacrifices of the Old Covenant, the tabernacle, the covenants God made with Israel. Since they had become Christians, had they lost all the blessings God had promised to give Israel? No! God showed them (and us!) that all blessings come through His well-beloved Son. He blesses Jews and Gentiles alike when they believe in Christ Jesus. To the Hebrew Christians, a beautiful promise was given: "Jesus Christ is the same yesterday, today, and forever" (Hebrews 13:8). He never changes. He is our Saviour, as well as theirs. He is the eternal God, the author of our salvation. (See Hebrews 12:2.) He is our Lord. He will be King of Israel and the entire world. What a wonderful Saviour He is!

Scripture to be studied: Hebrews 8:6-13; Ezekiel 34:11-16, 23-31; 37:1-14, 26-28

The *aim* of the lesson: To teach the blessings God has promised to Israel in the future.

What your students should *know*: The blessings of God come through the Lord Jesus Christ alone.

What your students should *feel*: A desire to have others share these blessings.

What your students should *do*: Tell others of God's love and forgiveness through the blood of Christ.

Lesson outline (for the teacher's and students' notebooks):
1. The New Covenant will be a covenant of peace (Ezekiel 34:11-16, 23-31).
2. The New Covenant will give life (Ezekiel 37:1-14).
3. Through the New Covenant Israel will know God (Ezekiel 37:26-28).
4. The New Covenant will be everlasting (Ezekiel 37:26).

The verses to be memorized:
> *God . . . [Who] brought again from the dead our Lord Jesus . . . through the blood of the everlasting covenant, make you perfect in every good work to do His will*
> (Hebrews 13:20, 21a)

THE LESSON

To make a covenant is a solemn act. Occasionally, two people when making a serious agreement, will prick their thumbs to make them bleed. On their written agreement, they make blood marks with their thumbs. Among tribes, men have been known to drink each other's blood to make a covenant final. By using blood, each is saying, "I promise with my life-blood never to change my mind about this agreement."

Hundreds of years before God gave the Old Covenant to His people, He made a solemn covenant with Abraham. God commanded him to kill three animals and two birds. (Much blood poured out that day!) The animals were to be divided and placed on the ground. God then put Abraham into a sound sleep and made a covenant with him. He told Abraham what He Himself intended to do. Abraham was not required to do anything. If Abraham had been commanded to do certain things as part of the agreement, he would have had to walk between the dead animals together with God. But God walked alone between the bodies. God Himself was promising to do what He said He would do. This was an unconditional covenant. (See Genesis 15:7-21.)

Later, when God gave his laws to the Israelites in the Old Covenant, they agreed to obey them. Their obedience was necessary for this was a conditional covenant. God would keep them safe and bless them if they obeyed Him and worshiped Him alone. God loved the Hebrew people and did many good things for them. They said they loved Him. They had promised to keep His rules. But they began breaking their part of the covenant almost immediately. As parents sometimes give their children another opportunity to be obedient, so God forgave His sinning people when they turned from their sinful ways. God again blessed them. But, alas, over and over they turned from God, choosing their own way, choosing to sin, choosing to worship other gods!

God punished His people by causing some to die. Others became prisoners in strange lands. But whenever they turned back to God and confessed their sins, He, their loving Father, took them back.

Show Illustration #9
God sent prophets to warn His people that they would be punished if they continued to disobey. The prophets preached also about God's promises. They explained about the wonderful things God would do for the Hebrews if they would truly love and obey Him.

Sometimes a father says to his son, "I shall not take any more of your disobedience. You must be punished." God had this same feeling when His people, the Jews, refused to accept His dear Son, the Lord Jesus Christ. God had sent Him for their good, to forgive their sins. Because they hated Him and put Him to death, the Old Covenant was completely broken. About 40 years later, God punished His people severely. He caused their enemies to destroy their beautiful city and magnificent temple of worship. Many Jews were killed. The rest were scattered throughout the world. And not only that, God had to put the nation of Israel aside. And today (almost 1900 years later) it is even yet set aside. All this time the Jews have not been like a special treasure to Him. What a long time to be punished for disobedience!

Show Illustration #11
God is always in control of everything. So He allowed the Lord Jesus to die. He, the one perfect Mediator between God and men, gave His own life-blood as a sacrifice for the sins of the world. Now the way was open for anyone Jew or non-Jew to become a child of God. Each one who trusts in Him becomes a chosen member of God's family.

The nation Israel has been set aside and is not now loving or worshiping the Son of God. Israel is not now receiving God's special favors. Only individual Jews who have received Christ as Saviour are receiving the blessings which all believers receive.

But God always keeps His promises. He has a perfect plan for everything. He promised to make a New Covenant with His people Israel and He will keep His promise. His new agreement with His people will be unconditional.

The Bible tells us that some things must happen before the New Covenant is final. First, the Lord Jesus will return in the air for His true church and take from the earth all whose trust is in Him. He will raise the dead believers and, together with those who are alive, they will be caught up to meet the Lord in the air. Seven years after this, the New Covenant with Israel will begin.

1. THE NEW COVENANT WILL BE A COVENANT OF PEACE
Ezekiel 34:11-16, 23-31

Show Illustration #13
Today the nation of Israel is like a large flock of sheep that has been scattered throughout many lands. The sheep need a shepherd. The Prophet Ezekiel wrote down the promises of God for Israel. "I will seek out My sheep . . . I will gather them from the countries . . . I will bring them to their own land . . . I will feed them in a good pasture . . . I will be their God . . . I will make a covenant of peace with them" (Ezekiel 34:11-25.)

Many Jews are now returning to the land of Israel. Many more will do so after the Church's rapture (when believers in Christ are caught up to meet the Lord in the air). While believers are with Christ in heaven, there will be seven years of terrible trouble and war here on earth. The people of Israel will suffer dreadfully. Then the Lord will bring about a great repentance among many of the Jews. (See Zechariah 12:10 13:2.) And Christ will suddenly return to the earth, right to the nation of Israel, right to their capital city, Jerusalem. Then He will be King of redeemed Israel and of the entire earth. He will destroy all their enemies. Israel will then be happy, peaceful, and a powerful nation. Just as God is the Great Shepherd of all believers today, He will lead and care for Israel when they receive the blessings of the New Covenant. (See Hebrews 13:20.)

2. THE NEW COVENANT WILL GIVE LIFE
Ezekiel 37:1-14

Show Illustration #14

God gave the Prophet Ezekiel quite an unusual picture to teach him more about the nation of Israel. God caused Ezekiel to see a valley covered with bones of dead men. But God caused the bones to come together. He put muscles on them and covered them with skin. Then He called for His Spirit to breathe on the dead bodies. As the breath of God went into them, they stood to their feet like a great army. The bones were alive!

God then taught Ezekiel what this picture meant. The nation had been separated from God. Spiritually, the nation is dead. But when Christ comes to be their King, the repentant part of the nation will be restored to life spiritually. They will believe in Christ as the Saviour. (See Romans 11:25-27.) God will forgive their sins as He forgives ours through the precious blood of Christ. God promises: "I shall put my Spirit in you and you will live" They had been a dead nation to God because of their sin. God also says: "I shall cleanse their sins. I shall be their God and they will be My people." Just as God helps us to become like Christ and do His will (Hebrews 13:20-21), so He will teach His people in that day to love Him and serve Him–after they receive Him.

3. THROUGH THE NEW COVENANT ISRAEL WILL KNOW GOD
Ezekiel 37:26-28

In the letter to the Hebrews, God speaks of the New Covenant which He has promised to Israel. ". . . I shall put My laws into their mind, and write them in their hearts . . . I shall be to them a God . . . they shall be to Me a people . . . all shall know Me, from the least to the greatest." (See Hebrews 8:7-13.)

Instead of God's laws being written on stone, He will write them on their hearts. And everyone, even the children, will know Him then.

Show Illustration #15

Under the Old Covenant, God's people were kept away from Him. Only the priests (the mediators) were allowed to go through the curtain into the tabernacle. Inside, the priests offered to God sacrifices for the sins of the people. Outside, they spoke to the people for God. When the Lord Jesus died on the cross (we are told in the letter to the Hebrews), He opened the new and living way to God. (See Hebrews 10:20.)

When Jesus returns, a large number of the Jewish people will finally turn to God. They will have to come the one and only way that all people today must come to Him. Each must believe that Jesus is God the Son who died for their sins. They must confess their sins to God and receive Christ as Saviour. (See John 14:6.)

4. THE NEW COVENANT WILL BE EVERLASTING
Ezekiel 37:26

Show Illustration #16

Long ago God promised, ". . . I shall make an everlasting covenant with Israel. . . . I shall put my fear in their hearts, that they shall not depart from me" (Jeremiah 32:40). God means it. He will never change His mind. He longs to have the Hebrew people turn from their sin to the Saviour. He wants them again as His special people.

Why is it important for us to know these things we have studied? Because God wants us to know Him. He wants us to know His Word and His plans. God has always known exactly what He was doing. He still knows. He planned that Jesus' blood would be the perfect sacrifice for sin forever. He wants us to know there is only one way to become a child of God, a believer in Christ. (See Hebrews 10:12-14.) He wants us to know that His promises in the Bible are for every believer, not only for Israel. He also wants us to know that we must tell others there is only one way to Him.

Many Jews will not be alive when Christ comes to set up His kingdom on earth. No one can count on living a certain length of time. So Jews and non-Jews all over the world must be told that Christ has opened the way for them to come to God. They must be told that the punishment for sin is death–separation from–God forever.

Are you explaining to others how they may go to heaven? Are you praying for those who have gone to tell the good news in faraway lands? None will escape the punishment for sin if they refuse to place their trust in the Saviour. Have you received Him?

www.ingramcontent.com/pod-product-compliance
Lightning Source LLC
Chambersburg PA
CBHW060806090426
42736CB00002B/174